THE **FIRST BOOK** OF

FIRST PRINTING

Library of Congress Catalog Card Number: 54-5991

Printed in the United States of America by Acweltone Corporation

Published in Canada by Ambassador Books, Ltd., Toronto 1, Ontario

Rhythms

By Langston Hughes

Pictures by Robin King

FRANKLIN WATTS, INC.

699 Madison Avenue, New York 21

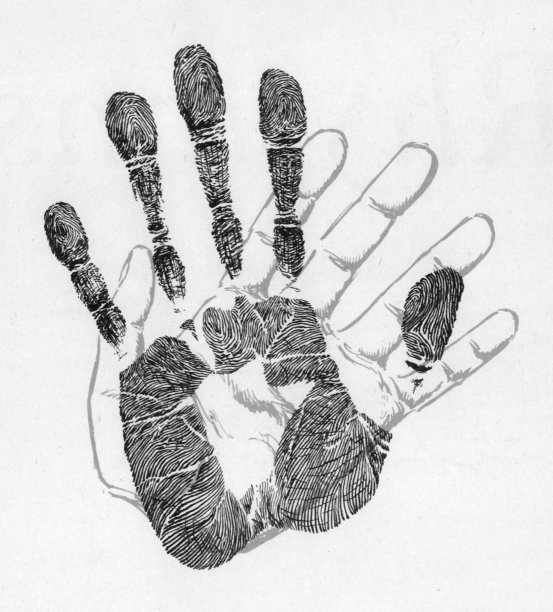

Contents

Let's Make a Rhythm

It is fun to start something.
Take a crayon or pencil and a
sheet of paper and start a line upward. Let it go up into a curve,
and you will have rhythm.
Then try a wavy line, and you will see how the
line itself seems to move.

2

Rhythm comes from movement. The motion of your pencil makes *your* line. When you lift your pencil as you finish, the rhythm of your line on the paper will be the rhythm of your hand in motion. Try this:

There is no rhythm in the world without movement first.

Make a point of a triangle, then a smaller one, then a smaller one than that, then a still smaller one, so that they keep on across a sheet of paper, all joined together.

Again you have made a rhythm. Your hand, your eye, and your pencil all moving together have made on the paper a rhythm that you can see with your eyes.

3

You can make a rhythm of sound by clapping your hands or tapping your foot. You can make a body rhythm by swaying your body from side to side or by making circles in the air with your arms.

Now make a large circle on a paper. Inside your circle make another circle. Inside that one make another one. See how these circles almost seem to move, for you have left something of your own movement there, and your own feeling of place and of roundness. Your circles are not quite like the circles of anyone else in the world, because you are not like anyone else. Your handwriting has a rhythm that is entirely your own. No one writes like anyone else.

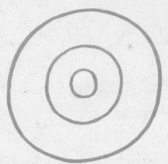

This is the way I write

How do you write?

Make a rhythm of peaks, starting from the bottom of one peak.

Make another rhythm like it, but start from the top.

Then do the same thing again, but put one rhythm over the other, and you have a pattern.

Fill in with your crayon and you have a pattern of diamond shapes. Rhythm makes patterns.

Draw a line. From the line make straight lines that slant up, each line growing a little longer. Or make another line and let the slanting lines cross it.

See how many rhythms you can make with straight lines,

with curving lines,

with circles overlapping circles,

and with circles around circles, starting with a dot.

If a friend is drawing with you, see how different your friend's circles are from your circles. It is fun to make something yourself with your *own* rhythm because it will always be different from what anyone else will make. Your circles and rhythms are yours alone.

The Beginnings of Rhythm

Your rhythm on this earth began first with the beat of your heart. The heart makes the blood flow. Feel your heart. Then feel your wrist where your pulse is. That is where you can best feel the rhythm of your blood moving through your body from the heart. Doctors measure the force of the blood with an instru-

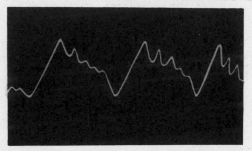

ment which pictures this rhythm in terms of the speed of its movement. The speed varies from person to person, but when a line is used to picture this movement, it looks in general like this.

Such a diagram-drawing is called a graph. This particular line, you see, has a definite, repeating rhythm as the pulse throbs to the flow of blood pumped by the heart. The rhythm of life is the beat of the heart. The beat of the heart makes a pattern seen on paper when it is recorded by what doctors call an electrocardio-

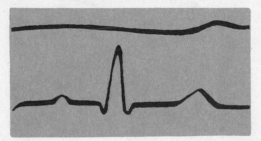

graph machine. Sometimes the pattern looks like this graph.

Listen to your heart. In most adults the heart beats about 72 times a minute, pumping blood through the heart into the canals of the body. When you run or when you are frightened, excited, or crying, your heart beats faster. Movement of the body, or the flow of thoughts or emotions through the mind, can change the rhythm of the heart for a while. Bad thoughts upset the heart. Happy thoughts do not disturb it unless they are sudden surprises. Usually, however, the heart pumps the same number of beats a minute, steadily, once a person becomes an adult, until he leaves our world. The rhythm of the heart is the first and most important rhythm of human life.

Thousands of years ago men transferred the rhythm of the heartbeat into a drumbeat, and the rhythm of music began. They made a slow steady drumbeat to walk to or march to, a faster beat to sing to, and a changing beat to dance to.

Try beating a slow steady rhythm with your fingers softly on the table, or on the edge of this book.

Try beating a changing rhythm that you can dance to.

Try beating the rhythm of a song you know, like "The Star-Spangled Banner."

Try clapping your hands in rhythm as people do for square dancing, the Charleston, or for games.

The rhythms of music start folks to feeling those rhythms in their minds and in their bodies. That is why music sometimes starts the heart beating faster. One rhythm may start another. The rhythm of the wind in the sky will change the movements of a kite floating in the air. The rhythm of water in the sea will make a boat rock faster or slower as the water moves. Rhythm begins in movement.

10

A little stream starts to flow down a mountainside from a new spring. It makes a path across the land as the water moves. Gradually the path is washed out deeper and deeper, following the course of the water's movement. If the stream keeps on flowing for a long time it will make a gully. Over the years it may even create a canyon by the rhythmical flowing of the water. Out of a wilderness of rock the steady flow of the Colorado River carved America's beautiful Grand Canyon in Arizona, until it became an immense rhythmical cleft across the land. Its rhythm began with the steady movement of the water of the river. Even, steady motion is rhythm.

Varying Rhythms

The Mississippi River flows in a slow rhythm to the sea. Niagara Falls tumbles in a swift roaring curve of rhythm over a shelf of rock from one lake to another—Lake Erie to Lake Ontario. Water from an old-fashioned hose makes a single rhythmical arch as it falls onto the grass. But a garden spray produces a hundred lines of graceful curving water.

Steady, even rhythms are the easiest to make, or to look at, or listen to, or rest by. The tick of a clock, always the same, will put you to sleep. If you bounce a ball in an even rhythm, it is easier to keep it going. To skip rope and not miss, partners must turn the rope with an even speed. A swing swoops up and down evenly as you pump it. Grandma rocks steadily, not jerkily, in her rocking chair.

But steady, even rhythms are not always the most exciting, or the most interesting. An even rhythm is restful.

But an uneven rhythm is more interesting because it seems to be changing, to be going somewhere, to be doing something.

This rhythm does not change.

But this one does.

Varying rhythms are more exciting. This is perhaps why your heart beats faster when you start to school for the first time or take a trip or move to a new house and the rhythms of daily life change. Or why, when the rhythms of music vary or grow more rapid as in Ravel's "Bolero," or when the sea waves pound faster and louder, or the wind blows more swiftly and the trees sway violently, your heart beats faster, too.

One rhythm affects another rhythm. If one partner turns the end of a rope faster, the other partner must turn faster, too, to keep up. Otherwise there will be no rhythm in the turning. When two people dance together, they must dance together in the same rhythm, or it is no fun for either.

14

But different rhythms may sometimes be combined with interest. Straight lines make a rhythm of their own.

But with them a flowing line may be coupled to make an interesting combination of rhythms, one crossing the other,

or one on top of the other,

or below the other.

There are many combinations of varying rhythms and actions. A merry-go-round goes round and round while the animals on it go up and down. If you have ever watched a sea gull flying you have noticed that it flaps its wings awhile, then glides awhile, then flaps awhile, then glides again. Flap, flap—glide—flap, flap —glide. See what other kinds of varying rhythms you can think of yourself.

Sources of Rhythm

Artists have used animals, trees, men, waves, flowers, and many other objects in nature for rhythms.

In France 25,000 years ago the cave men made animal drawings on the walls of their caves.

Later the flag lily, *fleur-de-lis*, became a rhythmical design that is the national symbol of France.

African artists a thousand years ago made beautiful masks with rhythmical lines.

In the sixteenth century a Spanish artist named El Greco sometimes made a man look like this.

And Picasso with a few lines
has made a bull like this.

An American artist named
Paul Manship made a figure of
a man in Rockefeller Plaza in
New York like this.

Each artist makes his own rhythms out of the things
he sees around him and sees in his dreams and mind.

17

The most beautiful rhythms seem always to be moving upward. That must be because the sun is above, and the growing things that start in the earth grow upward toward it.

A blade of grass moves upward as it grows. So does a flower, first only a little sprout, then a stem giving off other stems that turn into branches that bud as the plant grows taller. The buds turn into flowers as high above the earth and as near the sun as each plant can reach. Small plants like violets do not reach very high. Tall plants like sunflowers or hollyhocks sometimes grow taller than a man. Trees like magnolias bloom away up in the air. From the roots in the earth to the tallest flower, lines of rhythm flow upward. And in each leaf, each flower petal, there is rhythm. Nature is rhythm.

18

The lines of an oak leaf move outward and upward to its tip.

A locust leaf has rhythm, and a violet in bloom.

There is rhythm in a lily, and the bud of a rose before it opens much, and a many-petaled rose in full bloom.

Many vines curl upward. But some plants, like Spanish moss which lives on air, hang gracefully downward from the branches of trees. The leaves of water lilies float calmly on the surface of the water, but their blooms open toward the sun.

In growing things there is an endless variety of
rhythm from the shaggy, pyramiding pine to the tall
bare curve of a towering palm, from the trailing weep-
ing willow to the organ cactus of the desert, from the
straight loveliness of bamboo trees in the tropics to the
wind-shaped cypress of the California coast, clinging
to a rocky cliff near the sea where the waves shower
their salty spray.

20

This is one of the many rhythms of moving water in the sea.

These are some of the many thousands of rhythms that moisture makes when it forms a tiny snowflake, or when it becomes a ball of hail, or an icicle, or when it is just, as many poets have said, "the harp-strings of the rain."

Perhaps falling rain first gave men the idea of painting stripes as decoration on their walls or on their war shields, or of weaving stripes into their garments, or making a rhythm of slanting stripes that lean as rain sometimes does, or stripes flowing as rain in the wind may seem to flow and curve.

21

Perhaps the curve of a water-
fall or the arching stripes of the
rainbow suggested the rhythms
for the arches of the houses and
temples and tombs and bridges
of men long ago — the arch of Tamerlane's tomb at
Samarkand, the arch of a bridge in ancient China, or
the Moorish arches at Granada.

When the Egyptians built their tombs and temples over a thousand years before Christ, they knew how to combine the rhythms of nature with the possibilities of stone and sun-dried brick in the structure of their buildings. And the more harmoniously they did this, the more beautiful were their buildings. In splendid palaces the pharaohs lived.

The Greeks, hundreds of years before Christ, knew the rhythmical beauty of the soaring line in a column. The rising lines of its many columns made the Parthenon one of the most beautiful buildings ever created.

The columns of Greek temples go upward.

The pyramids of the Egyptians point upward.

The skyscrapers of American cities rise into the skies.

Like the blades of grass and the stems of flowers and the trunks of trees, the houses and temples and other buildings of man rise toward the sky where the sun is. Almost nobody builds a house, church, or any kind of building underground.

23

The Rhythms of Nature

From the motion of the planets around the sun — Old Sol — the rhythms of the sky are charted. The sun and the planets which move around it, with the moons, the comets, the meteors, and all the smaller asteroids too far away to be seen, are called the solar system.

24

You with your own eyes can watch the daily rhythm of night, day, night, day, night, day, and the rhythm of the four seasons that are spring, summer, fall, and winter, regularly repeating themselves over and over again. The rhythms of the moon becoming full, then waning, then becoming full again, you can see, too, as it revolves around the earth. The magnetic pull of these rhythms is recorded in the tides of the sea.

In nature many rhythms are related, one to another, and men and animals live according to these rhythms. Fields are planted in the spring, cultivated in summer, harvested in the fall, and the grain is stored for winter when the fields lie fallow. Some birds follow the seasons, flying south to keep up with the sun. All the planets move around the sun. All the rhythms of the part of the universe we know best are attuned to the sun. The rhythms of growing things almost always move upward toward the sun. Waves begin low in a trough of the sea and rise to a crest of foam.

The rhythms of the joyful spirit are rising ones. Animals in happiness leap upward. Ballet dancers rise as high as they can on their toes when dancing. Church steeples point toward the sky. When men pray their thoughts go up, and their souls are uplifted. When people are happy they generally walk with their heads up. When they are sad and days are dark and sunless, their heads are often down.

The sun influences the moon. The sun and moon influence the sea. The tides of the sea influence the shell life of the sea, and each shell is molded into a rhythmic shape of its own by all the rhythms and pressures that bear upon it from the sea. These are a few of the many shell shapes.

On the surface of each shell the lines of some additional rhythms are etched in graceful beauty.

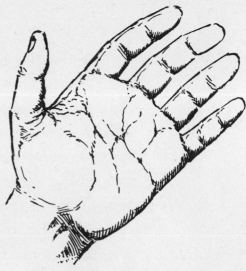

No one shell in the world is exactly like any other shell. There are millions of different shells. Even each shell of each family is different and the lines on each single shell are different, too.

You, like the shells, are like no one else. Even the rhythm of each line in your hands is like that in no one else's hands.

The rhythm of your walk is like no one else's walk. Some people walk with long easy steps, some trip along, some wobble. Soldiers learn to march in step together, with their walking rhythms at the same tempo, so that they all cover the same amount of ground in the same time at the same speed. They look better marching in rhythm. If one man gets out of step, he makes the whole company look bad. That is why all must follow the same marching rhythm. Forward, march! . . . One-two-three-four! . . . One-two-three-four!

At the Radio City Music Hall in New York there is a famous chorus of girl dancers called the Rockettes. Each girl's foot strikes the stage at the same time in rhythm when they are dancing. They are called precision dancers. When people are dancing together, the nearer their rhythms are alike, the better they look.

Rhythms of Music

Music sets the rhythm for dancing. The body follows the beat of the music. There are the fast whirl of the Viennese waltz, the skip and hop of the square dance, the glide of the fox trot, the step-step of the two-step, the fling of the Charleston with its flying legs, the prance of the old-fashioned cakewalk — each having its own style and rhythm. The first dances were done to the rhythms of the drums, long before other instruments were invented. And the tone of the drums and the volume of their sounds were molded by the rhythm of their shapes.

29

In America some of the happiest music for dancing is made by our jazz bands whose rhythms were born from the drums of Africa, and changed over to the piano, the trumpet, the bass viol, the saxophones, and all the other instruments that make up a band.

There is rhythm for dancing in words, too, like "Waltz me around again, Willie," the title of a song popular fifty years ago, which has a dancing sound.

The rhythms of music and of words cause people to want to move, or be moved, in time to them. Babies like to be bounced to

Bye, Baby Bunting,
Papa's gone a-hunting
To get a little rabbit skin
To wrap the Baby Bunting in.

Children dance to

Ring-around-the-rosy,
Pocket full of posy!

or play a game to

London Bridge is falling down,
Falling down, falling down!
London Bridge is falling down,
My fair lady!

In music there are simple rhythms and complicated rhythms. A popular song may follow the same rhythmical beat all the way through. In a symphony there may be many varied rhythms. The conductor of a large orchestra sets the tempo and controls the rhythms with the movement of his baton. If the men do not follow him the music is badly played and not pleasing. In the barnyard when animals are frightened and all the chickens start cackling, the dogs barking, ducks quacking, and cows mooing, each in different rhythms, the best way to describe the noise is by the word "pandemonium," which means a disorderly, inharmonious uproar. No one is moved by such noises.

But men are often moved by rhythmical music to work together better. Sailors on the old sailing ships sang sea chanteys as they hauled in the sails or lifted the anchor:

Heave-ho! Blow the man down!
Oh, give me some time to
Blow the man down!

Men plowing or sawing or breaking rock like to work to music, with the rhythm of the song matching the rhythm of their bodies as they work. In this song from the deep South the "Huh!" is where the men's breath comes out as their hammers hit the rock or their picks strike the earth:

I got a rainbow . . . Huh!
Round my shoulder . . . Huh!
Ain't gonna rain! . . . Huh!
Ain't gonna rain! . . . Huh!
This old hammer . . . Huh!
Killed John Henry . . . Huh!
Won't kill me, Lord! . . . Huh!
Won't kill me!

32

Rhythm makes it easier to use energy. Even sweeping a rug or raking a lawn is done better if the broom or rake is handled with a steady rhythmical motion. In countries where a farmer still harvests the grain by hand, he advances across the field with the rhythmical sweep of his scythe, and the grain falls before him. Often he sings as he mows. And at the end of the harvest all the farmers sing for fun.

Rhythm and Words

Even without music there is rhythm in verses like these:

Sing a song of sixpence
Pocket full of rye!
Four-and-twenty blackbirds
Baked into a pie.
When the pie was opened
The birds began to sing.
Wasn't that a dainty dish
To set before a king?

Rhythm is very much a part of poetry. Maybe that is because the first poems were songs. In ancient Greece poets made up words and tunes at the same time. In the Middle Ages bards and troubadours sang their poems. Nowadays poets usually make up only words. But behind the words of good poems there is always rhythm. These lines by William Blake have a fine rhythm:

Tiger! Tiger! Burning bright
In the forest of the night!

Even when poems do not rhyme there is rhythm,
as in the beautiful poetry of the Bible:

Whither thou goest, I will go,
And where thou lodgest, I will lodge.
Thy people shall be my people,
And thy God my God.

Or listen to the rolling lines of Walt Whitman:

In the dooryard fronting an old farmhouse near the white-washed
    palings,
Stands the lilac-bush tall-growing with heart-shaped leaves of rich
    green,
With many a pointed blossom rising delicate, with the perfume strong
    I love,
With every leaf a miracle . . . .

Stories and sermons and speeches and prayers have
their rhythms, too. How beautiful is the rhythm of
Lincoln's *Gettysburg Address:*

Fourscore and seven years ago our fathers brought forth on
this continent a new nation, conceived in liberty, and dedicated to
the proposition that all men are created equal.

Just as the feet of soldiers marching in rhythm carry men forward, so the rhythms of sermons or speeches or poems carry words marching into your mind in a way that helps you to remember them. That is why I think

To make words sing
Is a wonderful thing—
Because in a song
Words last so long.

Most of the rhythms men put into music and poetry may be found in nature: the drumming of the rain, the rap-rap-rapping of a woodpecker on a tree, the steady beat of the waves on the beach — breaking, retreating, breaking, retreating over and over again. The call of the whippoorwill, the bobolink, the oriole, the sparrow, the trilling song of the canary — all these helped men to form their own rhythms and make their first music.

Some Mysteries of Rhythm

Deep inside of men and animals there are other rhythms that we cannot explain, but that are a part of life. Nobody knows why, for example, different kinds of birds always build their own particular kind of nests, each with its own peculiar rhythmical shape.

A South American ovenbird's nest is always oven-shaped.

A Baltimore oriole's nest hangs down like a hammock.

Every worker honeybee that lives knows how to help build a honeycomb, and the cells of each comb are always the same shape and of the same two sizes.

White-faced hornets' nests are always like this.

How each new brood of birds or bees or hornets knows how to create the same patterns and the same rhythmical shapes we do not know, but we call it instinct. This is nature, handing down certain ways of living and rhythms of life from one generation to another. Old swallows and young swallows all swoop through the skies in the same arcs of motion, and wild geese always fly in the same V-formations. For some reason wild geese find it easier to fly in formation this way.

Men and women create rhythms that make things easier to do, too. In fact, some things could not get done at all without rhythm. If you live in the country, watch a farmer churning butter. If he does not churn with an even up-and-down rhythm there will be no butter. Watch your mother beating cake batter. If she beats this way, that way, then slow, then stopping, then fast, the cake will not come out a good one. But if she beats her batter with a steady rhythm everything is mixed well and it is a good cake.

39

Athletics

When you go to the circus and see a man or a woman in spangled tights swinging on a trapeze high at the top of the tent, you remember for a long time the thrill as the trapeze artist swoops gracefully into space. The rhythm of a swimmer leaping from a diving board, cutting through the air in the swift curve of a high dive, is a beautiful picture to remember, too. In the water, the swimmer with the smoothest and most harmonious rhythm to his strokes is the one who moves the fastest and most beautifully through the water.

The word "harmonious" is a part of the definitions of rhythm in most dictionaries. Rhythm is "an harmonious flow," says one. Another dictionary says that rhythm is the measure of time or movement by regular beats coming over and over again in harmonious relationship. A good athlete must have that harmony of movement or rhythm, which is called "form."

Notice the form of a championship baseball player. Pitchers like Allie Reynolds or Satchel Paige or Ewell Blackwell wind up for the pitch and let go with a rhythm that begins in the tips of their toes and ends at the tips of their fingers as it is transferred to the ball that speeds through the air.

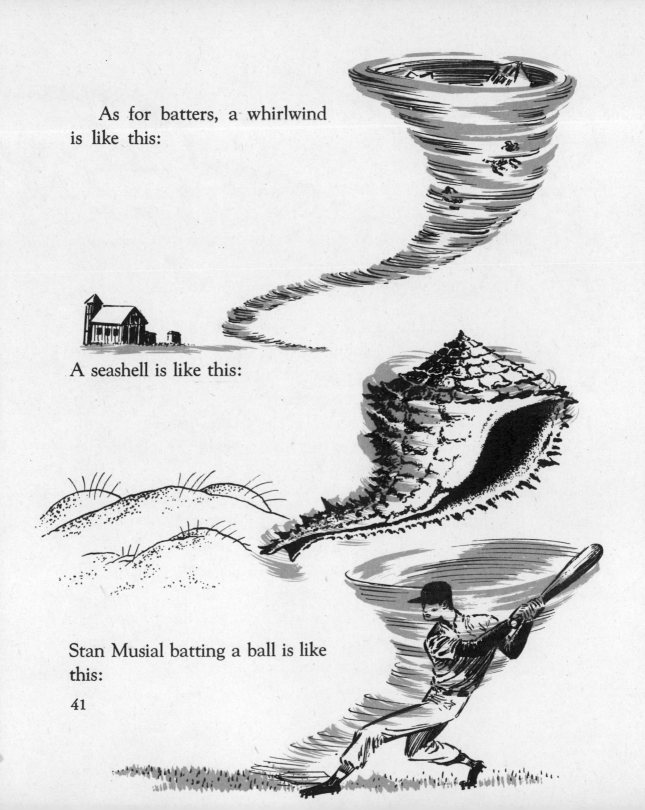

As for batters, a whirlwind is like this:

A seashell is like this:

Stan Musial batting a ball is like this:

41

Watch Johnny Mize or Ted Williams, Ralph Kiner — or yourself — for when you bat a ball, your whole body turns with the bat. A rhythm is set in motion that, in its turn, carries the ball, if you hit it well, in a curve through space. The ball makes its own rhythm in the air as it moves into the outfield. The outfielder leaps into the air like a bird as his hands go up to catch the ball. From pitch, to swing, to ball, a whole series of rhythms are set off, one rhythm, or one motion, starting another. So it is in life — from sun, to moon, to earth, to night, to day, to *you* getting up in the morning and going out to play a game of ball. *All* the rhythms of life in some way are related, one to another. You, your baseball, and the universe are brothers through rhythms.

Broken Rhythms

When rhythms between people are jerky and broken — for example, when friends quarrel — life is not happy. When you row a boat you cannot make much headway with short choppy strokes. But when your body bends to the strokes of the oars with a slow easy rhythm you can feel the transfer of your rhythm to the oars. Then the boat, too, takes on a rhythm and moves forward swiftly and smoothly through the water. People and races and nations get along better when they "row together."

When a sail is unfurled properly on a sailing ship and billows out as it catches the wind you can sense its rhythm and almost hear the music of its motion. You can almost see the wind in the canvas. When a kite flies you can feel at the string's end the way it is pulled by the wind. When you spin a top you can feel in your throwing of the top the way your rhythmical unfurling of the string changes into a hum and a whirl. When ballet dancers spin on their toes they spin in rhythm. If they do not, the results are ugly. Broken rhythms usually are not beautiful.

43

In 1910, the lines of automobiles were not as beautiful as the smoothly flowing lines of today's models, but were broken and full of angles. And even if they had had better motors these older automobiles with their clumsy, angular, broken rhythms could not have moved as fast as the new cars with their flowing lines, for the rhythms of shape are related to the rhythms of movement.

Machines

But new things are not always better than old things. The lines of a Grecian water jar made three thousand years ago are more beautiful than some modern water jugs. One reason is that in the old days more things were made by hand. Therefore many things were diffrent each from the other because each man, when making something, put into it his own individual rhythms.

Nowadays many things are made by machines that turn out thousands of copies, all just alike. When some of the long-ago Indians wove cloth by hand, each cloth was different and usually beautiful. Machines turn out

45

beautiful cloth, too, and more of it, faster, by making over and over the same copies. They may be beautiful copies *if the first designs are beautiful*. But a man or a woman must *first* design the cloth. Machines cannot create beauty. They can only copy it.

Machines move in rhythm. You can hear the rhythm of a printing press. You can see the rhythms of a generator in motion making energy to start, in turn, the motion of the machine it serves. You can see the rhythms of a piston, of a ramrod, of a shuttle, of a washing machine, of an egg beater, of a propeller.

46

An airplane propeller thrusts forward into currents of air and on the rhythms of the wind a plane rises into the sky. A Diesel engine turns its rhythms into power that carries a streamlined train rocking across the rails from city to distant city. The rhythm of a clock's balance wheel can be heard in its steady tick-tock, tick-tock, tick-tock. The rhythm of a steam shovel can be seen as it scoops up tons of earth.

47

Rhythms May Be Felt—and Smelled

The rhythms of the wind can be felt and certain sounds can be both felt and heard. An explosion at a distance can knock you down. Certain tones on the piano or violin hurt a dog's ears and will set him to howling. Some electronic vibrations, like those from short-wave radio transmitters, men cannot hear, but a dog can hear them, or feel them in his ears, and they hurt his eardrums. The vibrations from the sharp tone of a flute in a room have been known to break a pane of glass in a window. The flute player does not feel this tone from his flute, but it hits the pane of glass as hard as a stone, and the glass feels it. You cannot see electricity, but a shock can knock you down. Such an unseen rhythm may take on the force of a moving body. Perhaps tomorrow men may learn how to use such rhythms to shoot space ships to the moon.

In chemistry there are tiny bits of matter called molecules, too small for the eye to see. They move in a definite rhythm in liquids or gases, but we cannot see each tiny particle that makes up the gas. The air itself is gas, but we cannot see it. Instead we see *through* it.

Odors, or scents like those of perfumes, are really tiny particles, gases, or vapors in rhythmic motion. We smell them when they touch our noses although we cannot see them. In both chemistry and physics there are rhythms so complicated that it takes years of study to understand them. The rhythms of the patterns of light may be seen in colors called the spectrum. But there are many rhythms we cannot see, but which we can chart or measure.

Unseen Rhythms

Music may be heard, but not seen. It is true that the notes of music may be seen as written down on

paper. But notes serve only as a guide to sound. They mean very little until they are set in motion by the human voice or by instruments, to travel in rhythmical pulsations — like the beat of the pulse — to the ears of listeners. Sir Isaac Newton, who was a great pioneer in the science of modern physics, called sound "pulses of air." Sound cannot travel far alone, but from a radio tower, through the power of electronics, sound waves are transformed into electrical pulsations which go out on invisible electro-magnetic waves in every direction. Then people thousands of miles away can hear the sound by means of electronics. Our President can make a speech in Washington and folks across the ocean in London can hear him because of this marvelous modern science.

Electronics is the science of the movement of electro-magnetic waves. In broadcasting, these waves move outward and upward and around the earth through the air. They silently carry with them sound waves in electric pulsations which become audible words or music by means of our radio sets. They carry sights, too — unseen as they travel through space — which become pictures for our television screens. They create invisible radar guides which may direct an airplane through a fog to land, or keep a ship away from a reef.

There is an instrument called a phonodeik (FO-no-dike) for picturing the vibrations of sound waves as they travel.

This is the rhythm of a single tone in a soprano voice as it moves through the air.

This is a graph of the tone of a violin.

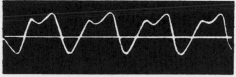

This is a bell tone.

And in the field of electronics, if the radar waves moving through space *could* be seen, they would look like this.

The rhythms of electronics were a mystery to men a hundred years ago. But now we know that light and sound and the force of the atom, too, each travels in its own series of rhythms. So, in this wonderful universe of ours there are rhythms that men can see, like those of sea waves. And there are unseen rhythms that we cannot see, but which we can chart and measure by scientific instruments and by mathematics. There remain to be solved tomorrow many fascinating mysteries about these unseen forces.

51

Rhythms in Daily Life

What is exciting about tomorrow is that it is always different from today. Back in the early 1900s the first airplane looked like a crate. But modern airplanes are streamlined.

To streamline something means to make the lines more rhythmical, more like a stream flowing. It is much more pleasing to look at a rhythmical, harmoniously shaped object than at an awkward thing. That is one reason industrial designers who create many of the things we use in daily life are paying more attention to rhythm and beauty.

Old - fashioned trains looked this way, and the coaches were rectangular.

New trains look like this.

The old ice box was shaped just like a box. But today's refrigerators are more graceful. And they are chilled by electricity from a dynamo whose power-rhythms are generated many miles away from your kitchen.

In grandma's day in the country, butter was put into a well to keep fresh. And cool water was drawn from the well in an "old oaken bucket." Thousands of years ago, before men learned to dig wells, they drank from springs or streams.

53

The first bowl to hold water was a man's cupped hand, or a pair of cupped hands.

Then the hands took clay and made a ball. A bowl is half of a ball, hollowed out. And a cup is just a bowl with a handle on it. A plate is just a bowl flattened out.

The first bowls and cups and plates were made only to be useful. Now we make them to be beautiful as well. Today fine designers like Russel Wright make beautiful dishes that are reproduced by machine methods so that people may buy them cheap. The rhythms of the hands of many makers of bowls, cups, glasses, and plates have given us the thousands of beautiful and useful shapes from which we eat and drink.

Furniture

It is interesting to observe the rhythms of furniture. The first chair was probably just a rock or a fallen log. Then a part of a log was set upright with a piece of the trunk left on it for a back. Then some planks were put together in angular fashion, very straight up and down.

Now chairs are made in many charming and graceful rhythms. Harmony or rhythm is very much a part of modern furniture-making.

55

And in our wallpaper and cloth, our towels and our curtains, our scarfs and neckties, the rhythms of lines and design are many. From the rhythms of nature — the pistil of a flower, the shape of an acorn, the tips of wheat stems — may come the designs on a man's tie, the patterns on living-room drapes, the border around your bedroom. At home, look and see what inspired the shapes and designs in your mother's wallpaper or the drapes at the windows.

How Rhythms Take Shape

Rhythms always follow certain conditions. Knitting creates its own rhythmical patterns by the very way the needles work in wool. So does chain stitching, cross-stitching, or featherstitching in sewing. Threads in weaving follow a rhythmical pattern according to the kind of weave being made. Pleats in dressmaking — knife pleats, accordion pleats — have a rhythm growing out of the way they are folded. When mothers curl little girls' hair they simply put the hair into the rhythm of spirals. But curls do not look well on all girls. Each person should arrange her hair to suit the shape of her face, just as a well-dressed woman chooses her hats to suit the lines of her profile, or her gowns to go well with the lines of her body.

57

Fashions in clothes and styles of decoration and design are everywhere influenced by other people and places around the world. That design on your father's tie may be from Persia. Your uncle's jacket is a Scotch plaid. The lines of your mother's dress are French. Her shawl is Spanish in design.

The music on your radio now is Cuban, its drums are the bongos of Africa, but the orchestra playing it is American. Rhythms go around the world, adopted and molded by other countries, mixing with other rhythms, and creating new rhythms as they travel.

58

In the Arctic the igloos make a curved rhythm against the sky. In America skyscrapers rear geometric towers above us. In Bechuanaland there are beehive huts, in Japan slant-roofed pagodas. Each building has its rhythms, loved by the people who made them, and often borrowed by others elsewhere. The Quonset hut of the American army is in shape not unlike an Eskimo igloo. And the East Indians are building skyscrapers in Bombay. We love Irish folk songs. The Irish love American jazz. Sometimes American jazz and Irish melodies combine to make a single song.

This Wonderful World

How wonderful are the rhythms of the world! Poets everywhere write about the drowsy hum of a bee. Farmers everywhere wake up to the cascade of a rooster's crow. In nature the rhythms we hear range from the trill of a bird to the chirp of a cricket, the lonely howl of a coyote to the thunderous roar of a lion, the gurgle of a brook to the boom of the sea, the purr of a cat to the beating of your own heart.

60

Look at the upward sweep of the horns of the antelope! See the outward curves of the Texas long-horned steer, the antlers of the elk, the stripes of the zebra or the tiger, the graceful neck of the giraffe, the delicate hoofs of a goat on a ledge, the curve of a sea lion on a rock, the scoop of a cat on a pillow, the flicker of a fish, the leap of a monkey, the wiggle of a puppy, the dive of a heron, the balance of hummingbirds, and butterflies, and ballet dancers, the drift of clouds across the sky in moving masses of vapor, the ever-spreading rhythm of the circles when you throw a stone into a pool of still water, the unseen rhythms of electronics that come right into your house bringing your favorite programs onto your TV screen! When a radio tower projects its electronic waves into the air, someone in Paris can hear a voice in New York saying, "Good morning"! Yet you cannot see or hear that voice on its way across the ocean. Such are the seen and the unseen, the heard and unheard rhythms of our world.

The earth which is our home moves in its own rhythm around the sun, as do all the planets. Animals, and boys and girls, and men and women, get up in the morning by the sun. Plants live by the sun. The moon moves around the earth as well as the sun. The rhythms of the sun and the moon influence the sea, the seasons, and us, and affect the rhythms of our universe, so immense in time and space that men do not yet understand most of it.